50 Swiss Chocolate Treat Recipes for Home

By: Kelly Johnson

Table of Contents

- Swiss Chocolate Truffles
- Swiss Chocolate Fondue
- Swiss Chocolate Cake
- Swiss Chocolate Mousse
- Swiss Chocolate Brownies
- Swiss Chocolate Bark
- Swiss Chocolate Soufflé
- Swiss Chocolate Chip Cookies
- Swiss Chocolate Hot Cocoa
- Swiss Chocolate Fudge
- Swiss Chocolate Éclairs
- Swiss Chocolate Cheesecake
- Swiss Chocolate Croissants
- Swiss Chocolate Tiramisu
- Swiss Chocolate Macarons
- Swiss Chocolate Bread Pudding
- Swiss Chocolate Pots de Crème
- Swiss Chocolate Dipped Strawberries
- Swiss Chocolate Pancakes
- Swiss Chocolate Ice Cream
- Swiss Chocolate Trifle
- Swiss Chocolate Biscotti
- Swiss Chocolate Lava Cake
- Swiss Chocolate Granola Bars
- Swiss Chocolate Pudding
- Swiss Chocolate Banana Bread
- Swiss Chocolate Cannoli
- Swiss Chocolate Marshmallows
- Swiss Chocolate Rice Krispie Treats
- Swiss Chocolate Panna Cotta
- Swiss Chocolate Caramel Slice
- Swiss Chocolate Nut Clusters
- Swiss Chocolate Crepes
- Swiss Chocolate Toffee
- Swiss Chocolate Coconut Balls

- Swiss Chocolate Chia Pudding
- Swiss Chocolate Caramel Popcorn
- Swiss Chocolate Raspberry Tart
- Swiss Chocolate Oatmeal Cookies
- Swiss Chocolate Hazelnut Spread
- Swiss Chocolate Mint Brownies
- Swiss Chocolate Almond Butter Cups
- Swiss Chocolate Shortbread
- Swiss Chocolate Liqueur Truffles
- Swiss Chocolate Brioche
- Swiss Chocolate Cherry Clafoutis
- Swiss Chocolate Cinnamon Rolls
- Swiss Chocolate Pecan Pie
- Swiss Chocolate Banana Split
- Swiss Chocolate Peanut Butter Bars

Swiss Chocolate Truffles

Ingredients:

- 200g Swiss dark chocolate, finely chopped
- 120ml heavy cream
- 30g unsalted butter
- 1 teaspoon vanilla extract
- Cocoa powder, powdered sugar, or chopped nuts for coating (optional)

Instructions:

In a small saucepan, heat the heavy cream over medium heat until it just begins to simmer.
Remove the cream from heat and add the finely chopped Swiss dark chocolate to the saucepan. Let it sit for 1-2 minutes.
Gently stir the chocolate and cream together until the chocolate is completely melted and the mixture is smooth.
Add the unsalted butter and vanilla extract to the chocolate mixture, stirring until the butter is melted and fully incorporated.
Transfer the chocolate ganache mixture to a bowl and cover it with plastic wrap. Chill in the refrigerator for at least 2 hours, or until the ganache is firm.
Once the ganache has chilled and firmed up, use a spoon or a small cookie scoop to scoop out portions of the ganache. Roll each portion between your palms to form small balls.
If desired, roll the chocolate truffles in cocoa powder, powdered sugar, or chopped nuts to coat them.
Place the coated truffles on a baking sheet lined with parchment paper and return them to the refrigerator to chill for another 30 minutes to set.
Once set, serve the Swiss chocolate truffles at room temperature. Enjoy!

Note: You can store the truffles in an airtight container in the refrigerator for up to two weeks. Allow them to come to room temperature before serving for the best taste and texture.

Swiss Chocolate Fondue

Ingredients:

- 200g Swiss dark chocolate, finely chopped
- 120ml heavy cream
- 1 tablespoon unsalted butter
- 1 teaspoon vanilla extract
- Assorted dippers (strawberries, bananas, pineapple, marshmallows, pound cake, etc.)

Instructions:

In a small saucepan, heat the heavy cream over medium heat until it just begins to simmer.
Remove the cream from heat and add the finely chopped Swiss dark chocolate to the saucepan. Let it sit for 1-2 minutes.
Gently stir the chocolate and cream together until the chocolate is completely melted and the mixture is smooth.
Stir in the unsalted butter and vanilla extract until the butter is melted and fully incorporated.
Transfer the chocolate fondue mixture to a fondue pot or a heatproof serving bowl.
Light the fondue burner or keep the heat source under the fondue pot on low to keep the chocolate warm and melted.
Arrange the assorted dippers on a platter or individual plates around the fondue pot.
Use fondue forks or skewers to dip the dippers into the melted chocolate, swirling to coat them fully.
Enjoy the Swiss chocolate fondue with your favorite dippers!

Note: If the fondue starts to thicken too much as it sits, you can stir in a splash of additional heavy cream to thin it out. Be careful not to overheat the fondue, as it can scorch or seize if it gets too hot. Adjust the heat source as needed to keep the fondue warm and smooth.

Swiss Chocolate Cake

Ingredients:

For the cake:

- 1 and 3/4 cups (220g) all-purpose flour
- 3/4 cup (75g) unsweetened cocoa powder
- 1 and 1/2 teaspoons baking powder
- 1 and 1/2 teaspoons baking soda
- 1/2 teaspoon salt
- 2 cups (400g) granulated sugar
- 2 large eggs
- 1 cup (240ml) whole milk
- 1/2 cup (120ml) vegetable oil
- 2 teaspoons vanilla extract
- 1 cup (240ml) boiling water

For the Swiss chocolate buttercream frosting:

- 1 cup (230g) unsalted butter, softened
- 3 and 1/2 cups (420g) powdered sugar, sifted
- 1/2 cup (50g) unsweetened cocoa powder, sifted
- 1 teaspoon vanilla extract
- 2-3 tablespoons heavy cream or milk
- Pinch of salt

For garnish (optional):

- Swiss chocolate shavings or curls

Instructions:

Preheat your oven to 350°F (175°C). Grease and flour two 9-inch round cake pans or line them with parchment paper.
In a large mixing bowl, sift together the flour, cocoa powder, baking powder, baking soda, and salt. Add the granulated sugar and whisk until well combined.

In a separate bowl, whisk together the eggs, milk, vegetable oil, and vanilla extract until smooth.

Gradually add the wet ingredients to the dry ingredients, mixing until just combined. Be careful not to overmix.

Slowly pour in the boiling water and stir until the batter is well combined and smooth. The batter will be thin, but that's normal.

Divide the batter evenly between the prepared cake pans.

Bake in the preheated oven for 30-35 minutes, or until a toothpick inserted into the center of the cakes comes out clean.

Remove the cakes from the oven and allow them to cool in the pans for about 10 minutes before transferring them to a wire rack to cool completely.

While the cakes are cooling, prepare the Swiss chocolate buttercream frosting. In a large mixing bowl, beat the softened butter until creamy and smooth.

Gradually add the sifted powdered sugar and cocoa powder, mixing on low speed until well combined.

Add the vanilla extract, heavy cream or milk, and a pinch of salt. Beat on medium-high speed until the frosting is smooth and fluffy, adding more cream or milk as needed to achieve the desired consistency.

Once the cakes are completely cooled, place one layer on a serving plate or cake stand. Spread a layer of the chocolate buttercream frosting evenly over the top. Place the second cake layer on top and frost the top and sides of the cake with the remaining frosting.

Garnish with Swiss chocolate shavings or curls, if desired.

Slice and serve the Swiss chocolate cake, and enjoy!

Note: Store any leftover cake in an airtight container in the refrigerator for up to 3-4 days. Bring the cake to room temperature before serving for the best taste and texture.

Swiss Chocolate Mousse

Ingredients:

- 200g Swiss dark chocolate, finely chopped
- 3 large eggs, separated
- 1/4 cup (50g) granulated sugar
- 1 teaspoon vanilla extract
- Pinch of salt
- 1 cup (240ml) heavy cream

Instructions:

Melt the Swiss dark chocolate: Place the finely chopped chocolate in a heatproof bowl. Set the bowl over a pot of simmering water (double boiler method), ensuring the bottom of the bowl doesn't touch the water. Stir the chocolate occasionally until melted and smooth. Remove from heat and let it cool slightly.
In a separate mixing bowl, beat the egg yolks with the granulated sugar and vanilla extract until pale and creamy.
Gradually pour the melted chocolate into the egg yolk mixture, stirring continuously until well combined. Set aside.
In another clean mixing bowl, beat the egg whites with a pinch of salt until stiff peaks form.
In a separate bowl, whip the heavy cream until soft peaks form.
Gently fold the whipped cream into the chocolate mixture until evenly combined.
Next, fold in the beaten egg whites in two batches, being careful not to deflate the mixture.
Once fully incorporated, spoon the Swiss chocolate mousse into individual serving glasses or bowls.
Chill the mousse in the refrigerator for at least 2-3 hours, or until set.
Serve the Swiss chocolate mousse chilled, optionally garnished with whipped cream, chocolate shavings, or fresh berries.
Enjoy the rich and decadent Swiss chocolate mousse!

Swiss Chocolate Brownies

Ingredients:

- 200g Swiss dark chocolate, finely chopped
- 1/2 cup (115g) unsalted butter
- 3/4 cup (150g) granulated sugar
- 2 large eggs
- 1 teaspoon vanilla extract
- 1/2 cup (60g) all-purpose flour
- 2 tablespoons unsweetened cocoa powder
- 1/4 teaspoon salt
- 1/2 cup (60g) chopped nuts (optional)

Instructions:

Preheat your oven to 350°F (175°C). Grease and line an 8x8-inch (20x20cm) baking pan with parchment paper, leaving an overhang on the sides for easy removal.
In a heatproof bowl, combine the finely chopped Swiss dark chocolate and unsalted butter. Melt the chocolate and butter together using a double boiler or by microwaving in 30-second intervals, stirring until smooth. Set aside to cool slightly.
In a separate mixing bowl, whisk together the granulated sugar, eggs, and vanilla extract until well combined.
Pour the melted chocolate mixture into the egg mixture and whisk until smooth and evenly combined.
Sift in the all-purpose flour, cocoa powder, and salt. Use a spatula or wooden spoon to gently fold the dry ingredients into the wet ingredients until just combined. Be careful not to overmix.
If desired, fold in the chopped nuts until evenly distributed throughout the batter.
Pour the batter into the prepared baking pan and spread it out evenly using a spatula.
Bake in the preheated oven for 25-30 minutes, or until a toothpick inserted into the center comes out with a few moist crumbs attached.
Remove the brownies from the oven and allow them to cool completely in the pan set on a wire rack.

Once cooled, lift the brownies out of the pan using the parchment paper overhang and transfer them to a cutting board.
Use a sharp knife to cut the brownies into squares or rectangles.
Serve the Swiss chocolate brownies and enjoy them with a glass of milk or a scoop of ice cream, if desired.
Store any leftovers in an airtight container at room temperature for up to 3-4 days.

Enjoy these decadent Swiss chocolate brownies!

Swiss Chocolate Bark

Ingredients:

- 200g Swiss dark chocolate, finely chopped
- 1/2 cup (60g) chopped nuts (e.g., almonds, pistachios, walnuts)
- 1/4 cup (30g) dried fruit (e.g., cranberries, cherries, apricots)
- 1/4 cup (40g) mixed seeds (e.g., pumpkin seeds, sunflower seeds)
- Pinch of sea salt (optional)

Instructions:

Line a baking sheet with parchment paper or a silicone baking mat.

In a heatproof bowl, melt the Swiss dark chocolate using a double boiler or by microwaving in 30-second intervals, stirring until smooth.

Once the chocolate is melted, pour it onto the prepared baking sheet. Use a spatula to spread the chocolate into an even layer, about 1/4 inch (0.6 cm) thick.

Sprinkle the chopped nuts, dried fruit, and mixed seeds evenly over the melted chocolate. Gently press them down into the chocolate using the back of a spoon or spatula.

If desired, sprinkle a pinch of sea salt over the top of the chocolate bark for a sweet and salty contrast.

Place the baking sheet in the refrigerator for about 30 minutes, or until the chocolate is set and firm.

Once set, remove the chocolate bark from the refrigerator and break it into pieces using your hands or a sharp knife.

Serve the Swiss chocolate bark as a delicious snack or dessert.

Store any leftover chocolate bark in an airtight container at room temperature for up to 1 week, or in the refrigerator for longer shelf life.

Enjoy this simple and customizable Swiss chocolate bark!

Swiss Chocolate Soufflé

Ingredients:

- 200g Swiss dark chocolate, finely chopped
- 3 large egg yolks
- 4 large egg whites
- 1/4 cup (50g) granulated sugar, plus extra for coating ramekins
- 1/4 cup (60ml) heavy cream
- 1/2 teaspoon vanilla extract
- Pinch of salt
- Butter or non-stick cooking spray, for greasing ramekins

Instructions:

Preheat your oven to 375°F (190°C). Place a baking sheet in the oven to preheat as well. Grease the bottoms and sides of four 6-ounce (180ml) ramekins with butter or non-stick cooking spray. Sprinkle granulated sugar into each ramekin, tilting and rotating them to coat the bottoms and sides evenly. Discard any excess sugar.

In a heatproof bowl set over a pot of simmering water (double boiler), melt the Swiss dark chocolate, stirring occasionally until smooth. Remove from heat and let it cool slightly.

In a separate bowl, whisk together the egg yolks, heavy cream, and vanilla extract until well combined.

Gradually whisk the egg yolk mixture into the melted chocolate until smooth and evenly combined.

In a clean, dry mixing bowl, use an electric mixer to beat the egg whites and salt until soft peaks form. Gradually add the granulated sugar, a little at a time, and continue beating until stiff, glossy peaks form.

Gently fold about one-third of the beaten egg whites into the chocolate mixture to lighten it. Then, carefully fold in the remaining egg whites in two additions, being careful not to deflate the mixture.

Divide the soufflé mixture evenly among the prepared ramekins, filling each one almost to the top.

Run your thumb around the inside edge of each ramekin to create a slight indentation, which helps the soufflés rise evenly.

Place the filled ramekins on the preheated baking sheet in the oven. Bake for 12-15 minutes, or until the soufflés are puffed up and set around the edges but still slightly jiggly in the center.

Remove the soufflés from the oven and serve immediately, as they will begin to deflate shortly after baking.

Optionally, dust the tops of the soufflés with powdered sugar before serving.

Enjoy the light and fluffy Swiss chocolate soufflés as a decadent dessert!

Note: Be sure to serve the soufflés immediately after baking, as they will begin to deflate shortly after coming out of the oven.

Swiss Chocolate Chip Cookies

Ingredients:

- 1 cup (226g) unsalted butter, softened
- 3/4 cup (150g) granulated sugar
- 3/4 cup (150g) packed light brown sugar
- 2 large eggs
- 1 teaspoon vanilla extract
- 2 and 1/4 cups (281g) all-purpose flour
- 1 teaspoon baking soda
- 1/2 teaspoon salt
- 2 cups (340g) Swiss chocolate chips or chunks

Instructions:

Preheat your oven to 375°F (190°C). Line baking sheets with parchment paper or silicone baking mats.
In a large mixing bowl, cream together the softened unsalted butter, granulated sugar, and brown sugar until light and fluffy.
Add the eggs, one at a time, beating well after each addition. Mix in the vanilla extract until well combined.
In a separate bowl, whisk together the all-purpose flour, baking soda, and salt.
Gradually add the dry ingredients to the wet ingredients, mixing until just combined.
Fold in the Swiss chocolate chips or chunks until evenly distributed throughout the cookie dough.
Drop tablespoon-sized portions of dough onto the prepared baking sheets, spacing them about 2 inches apart.
Bake in the preheated oven for 8-10 minutes, or until the edges are lightly golden brown.
Remove the cookies from the oven and let them cool on the baking sheets for a few minutes before transferring them to wire racks to cool completely.
Once cooled, store the Swiss chocolate chip cookies in an airtight container at room temperature.
Enjoy these delicious cookies with a glass of milk or a cup of coffee!

Note: Feel free to adjust the amount of chocolate chips or chunks according to your preference. You can also add chopped nuts or other mix-ins if desired.

Swiss Chocolate Hot Cocoa

Ingredients:

- 2 cups (480ml) whole milk
- 1/4 cup (60ml) heavy cream
- 100g Swiss dark chocolate, finely chopped
- 2 tablespoons granulated sugar (adjust to taste)
- 1/2 teaspoon vanilla extract
- Pinch of salt
- Whipped cream, marshmallows, or chocolate shavings for topping (optional)

Instructions:

In a small saucepan, combine the whole milk and heavy cream. Heat the mixture over medium heat until it begins to simmer, but do not let it boil.
Once the milk mixture is simmering, reduce the heat to low and add the finely chopped Swiss dark chocolate to the saucepan.
Whisk continuously until the chocolate is completely melted and the mixture is smooth and creamy.
Stir in the granulated sugar, vanilla extract, and a pinch of salt. Adjust the sweetness to taste, adding more sugar if desired.
Continue to heat the hot cocoa for another 1-2 minutes, stirring occasionally, until it is hot and thoroughly combined.
Remove the saucepan from the heat and pour the hot cocoa into mugs.
If desired, top each mug with whipped cream, marshmallows, or chocolate shavings.
Serve the Swiss chocolate hot cocoa immediately and enjoy its rich, indulgent flavor!

Note: You can customize this hot cocoa recipe by adding a dash of cinnamon, nutmeg, or peppermint extract for extra flavor. Adjust the amount of chocolate or sugar according to your preference.

Swiss Chocolate Fudge

Ingredients:

- 400g Swiss dark chocolate, chopped
- 1 can (14 oz) sweetened condensed milk
- 1/4 cup (60g) unsalted butter
- 1 teaspoon vanilla extract
- Pinch of salt
- Optional toppings: chopped nuts, sea salt flakes, shredded coconut

Instructions:

Line an 8x8 inch (20x20 cm) baking dish with parchment paper, leaving some overhang on the sides for easy removal of the fudge.

In a saucepan over low heat, combine the chopped Swiss dark chocolate, sweetened condensed milk, and unsalted butter. Stir continuously until the chocolate and butter are melted and the mixture is smooth and well combined.

Once the mixture is smooth, remove the saucepan from the heat and stir in the vanilla extract and a pinch of salt.

Pour the chocolate mixture into the prepared baking dish, spreading it out evenly with a spatula.

If desired, sprinkle your choice of toppings over the surface of the fudge, gently pressing them down with the back of a spoon or spatula.

Place the baking dish in the refrigerator and chill the fudge for at least 2-3 hours, or until set.

Once the fudge is set, lift it out of the baking dish using the parchment paper overhang and transfer it to a cutting board.

Use a sharp knife to cut the fudge into squares or rectangles.

Serve the Swiss chocolate fudge at room temperature and enjoy!

Store any leftover fudge in an airtight container in the refrigerator for up to two weeks.

Enjoy the rich and decadent Swiss chocolate fudge as a delicious treat or homemade gift!

Swiss Chocolate Éclairs

Ingredients:

For the choux pastry:

- 1/2 cup (120ml) water
- 1/4 cup (60g) unsalted butter
- 1/2 cup (60g) all-purpose flour
- 2 large eggs

For the chocolate pastry cream filling:

- 1 cup (240ml) whole milk
- 3 large egg yolks
- 1/4 cup (50g) granulated sugar
- 2 tablespoons (15g) cornstarch
- 1 teaspoon vanilla extract
- 100g Swiss dark chocolate, chopped

For the chocolate glaze:

- 100g Swiss dark chocolate, chopped
- 1/4 cup (60ml) heavy cream
- 1 tablespoon unsalted butter

Instructions:

Preheat your oven to 400°F (200°C). Line a baking sheet with parchment paper. To make the choux pastry, in a saucepan, combine the water and butter over medium heat. Bring to a boil, then remove from heat and quickly stir in the flour until a smooth dough forms.
Return the saucepan to low heat and continue stirring the dough for about 1-2 minutes to dry it out slightly.
Transfer the dough to a mixing bowl and let it cool for a few minutes. Then, beat in the eggs one at a time, mixing well after each addition, until you have a smooth, shiny dough.

Transfer the choux pastry dough to a piping bag fitted with a large round tip. Pipe the dough onto the prepared baking sheet in long strips, about 4 inches long and 1 inch wide, leaving space between each éclair.

Bake the éclairs in the preheated oven for 15-20 minutes, or until puffed and golden brown. Reduce the oven temperature to 350°F (180°C) and continue baking for an additional 10 minutes to dry out the centers. Remove from the oven and let them cool completely on a wire rack.

To make the chocolate pastry cream filling, heat the milk in a saucepan over medium heat until it just begins to simmer.

In a mixing bowl, whisk together the egg yolks, sugar, and cornstarch until pale and creamy.

Gradually pour the hot milk into the egg yolk mixture, whisking constantly to temper the eggs.

Return the mixture to the saucepan and cook over medium heat, stirring constantly, until thickened. Remove from heat and stir in the vanilla extract and chopped Swiss dark chocolate until smooth and well combined. Let the pastry cream cool to room temperature.

Once the éclairs and chocolate pastry cream are cooled, use a sharp knife to make a small slit in the side of each éclair. Fill a piping bag fitted with a small round tip with the chocolate pastry cream and pipe it into the éclairs.

To make the chocolate glaze, heat the heavy cream in a saucepan over medium heat until it just begins to simmer. Remove from heat and stir in the chopped Swiss dark chocolate and unsalted butter until smooth and glossy.

Dip the top of each filled éclair into the chocolate glaze, allowing any excess to drip off. Place them on a wire rack to set.

Serve the Swiss chocolate éclairs chilled or at room temperature. Enjoy the decadent treat!

Store any leftover éclairs in an airtight container in the refrigerator for up to 2 days.

Swiss Chocolate Cheesecake

Ingredients:

For the crust:

- 1 and 1/2 cups (150g) chocolate cookie crumbs
- 1/4 cup (50g) granulated sugar
- 6 tablespoons (85g) unsalted butter, melted

For the filling:

- 400g Swiss dark chocolate, finely chopped
- 24 oz (680g) cream cheese, softened
- 1 cup (200g) granulated sugar
- 4 large eggs
- 1 teaspoon vanilla extract
- 1/2 cup (120ml) heavy cream

For the topping (optional):

- Whipped cream
- Chocolate shavings or cocoa powder

Instructions:

Preheat your oven to 350°F (175°C). Grease a 9-inch (23cm) springform pan and wrap the bottom with aluminum foil to prevent leaks.
In a mixing bowl, combine the chocolate cookie crumbs, granulated sugar, and melted butter. Mix until the crumbs are evenly moistened.
Press the mixture into the bottom of the prepared springform pan, using the back of a spoon or your fingers to create an even layer. Bake the crust in the preheated oven for 10 minutes, then remove and let it cool while you prepare the filling.
In a heatproof bowl set over a pot of simmering water (double boiler), melt the Swiss dark chocolate, stirring occasionally until smooth. Remove from heat and let it cool slightly.
In a large mixing bowl, beat the softened cream cheese and granulated sugar until smooth and creamy.
Add the eggs one at a time, mixing well after each addition. Stir in the vanilla extract.

Gradually pour in the melted chocolate while mixing on low speed, until fully incorporated.

Finally, add the heavy cream and mix until the batter is smooth and well combined.

Pour the filling over the cooled crust in the springform pan, spreading it out evenly with a spatula.

Place the springform pan in a larger roasting pan and fill the roasting pan with hot water until it reaches about halfway up the sides of the springform pan. This water bath helps prevent cracks on the surface of the cheesecake.

Bake the cheesecake in the preheated oven for 55-60 minutes, or until the edges are set and the center is slightly jiggly.

Turn off the oven and leave the cheesecake inside with the door slightly ajar for about 1 hour to cool gradually. Then, remove the cheesecake from the oven and let it cool completely at room temperature.

Once cooled, refrigerate the cheesecake for at least 4 hours, or preferably overnight, to set completely.

Before serving, optionally garnish the cheesecake with whipped cream and chocolate shavings or cocoa powder.

Slice and serve the Swiss chocolate cheesecake chilled. Enjoy the rich and indulgent dessert!

Swiss Chocolate Croissants

Ingredients:

- 1 sheet of frozen puff pastry, thawed
- 100g Swiss dark chocolate, chopped into small pieces
- 1 egg, beaten (for egg wash)
- Powdered sugar, for dusting (optional)

Instructions:

Preheat your oven to 400°F (200°C). Line a baking sheet with parchment paper or silicone baking mat.

Unfold the thawed puff pastry sheet onto a lightly floured surface. Use a rolling pin to gently roll out the pastry to smooth out any creases and create an even rectangle.

Use a sharp knife or pizza cutter to cut the pastry into triangles. You can adjust the size of the triangles based on how large you want your croissants to be.

Place a small handful of chopped Swiss dark chocolate at the base of each triangle, then roll up the triangles, starting from the base and rolling towards the tip, to form croissants.

Arrange the chocolate-filled croissants on the prepared baking sheet, leaving some space between each one.

Brush the tops of the croissants with beaten egg, using a pastry brush. This will give them a golden-brown finish when baked.

Bake the chocolate croissants in the preheated oven for 15-20 minutes, or until they are puffed up and golden brown.

Remove the croissants from the oven and let them cool on the baking sheet for a few minutes before transferring them to a wire rack to cool completely.

Once cooled, you can dust the chocolate croissants with powdered sugar for an extra touch of sweetness, if desired.

Serve the Swiss chocolate croissants warm or at room temperature, and enjoy the delightful combination of flaky pastry and gooey chocolate filling!

Store any leftover croissants in an airtight container at room temperature for up to 2 days, or freeze them for longer storage. Reheat frozen croissants in a preheated oven until warmed through before serving.

Swiss Chocolate Tiramisu

Ingredients:

- 2 cups (480ml) brewed coffee, cooled
- 3 tablespoons coffee liqueur (e.g., Kahlua), optional
- 200g Swiss dark chocolate, finely chopped
- 4 large eggs, separated
- 1/2 cup (100g) granulated sugar
- 1 teaspoon vanilla extract
- 8 oz (227g) mascarpone cheese, softened
- 1 cup (240ml) heavy cream
- 24-30 ladyfinger cookies (savoiardi)
- Cocoa powder, for dusting

Instructions:

In a shallow dish, combine the brewed coffee and coffee liqueur (if using). Set aside.
Melt the Swiss dark chocolate in a heatproof bowl set over a pot of simmering water (double boiler method). Once melted, set aside to cool slightly.
In a large mixing bowl, beat the egg yolks and granulated sugar until pale and creamy. Stir in the vanilla extract and melted chocolate until well combined.
Add the softened mascarpone cheese to the chocolate mixture and beat until smooth and creamy.
In a separate mixing bowl, whip the heavy cream until stiff peaks form.
Gently fold the whipped cream into the chocolate mascarpone mixture until well incorporated.
In another clean mixing bowl, beat the egg whites until stiff peaks form.
Gently fold the beaten egg whites into the chocolate mascarpone mixture until no streaks remain.
Dip each ladyfinger cookie into the coffee mixture briefly, ensuring they are soaked but not soggy. Arrange a layer of soaked ladyfingers in the bottom of a 9x13-inch (23x33cm) baking dish or a similar-sized serving dish.
Spread half of the chocolate mascarpone mixture evenly over the layer of soaked ladyfingers.
Repeat the layers with another layer of soaked ladyfingers followed by the remaining chocolate mascarpone mixture.

Cover the tiramisu with plastic wrap and refrigerate for at least 4 hours, or preferably overnight, to allow the flavors to meld and the dessert to set.
Before serving, dust the top of the tiramisu with cocoa powder using a fine-mesh sieve.
Slice and serve the Swiss chocolate tiramisu chilled, and enjoy the rich and indulgent flavors!
Store any leftover tiramisu in the refrigerator for up to 2-3 days.

Swiss Chocolate Macarons

Ingredients:

For the macaron shells:

- 100g Swiss dark chocolate, finely chopped
- 1 cup (100g) almond flour
- 1 and 1/2 cups (180g) powdered sugar
- 2 large egg whites, at room temperature
- 1/4 cup (50g) granulated sugar
- Pinch of salt
- Swiss chocolate ganache (recipe below), for filling

For the Swiss chocolate ganache:

- 100g Swiss dark chocolate, finely chopped
- 1/2 cup (120ml) heavy cream
- 1 tablespoon unsalted butter

Instructions:

Prepare the Swiss chocolate ganache: In a heatproof bowl, place the finely chopped Swiss dark chocolate. In a small saucepan, heat the heavy cream over medium heat until it just begins to simmer. Pour the hot cream over the chopped chocolate and let it sit for 1-2 minutes. Stir until the chocolate is completely melted and smooth. Add the unsalted butter and stir until incorporated. Let the ganache cool to room temperature.

Line two baking sheets with parchment paper or silicone baking mats. Prepare a piping bag with a round tip (about 1/2 inch in diameter).

In a food processor, combine the almond flour and powdered sugar. Pulse several times until well combined and any large lumps are broken up. Sift the mixture through a fine-mesh sieve into a large mixing bowl.

In a separate clean mixing bowl, beat the egg whites with a pinch of salt on medium speed until foamy. Gradually add the granulated sugar, a little at a time, while continuing to beat. Increase the speed to high and beat until stiff, glossy peaks form.

Add about one-third of the beaten egg whites to the almond flour mixture. Using a spatula, gently fold the egg whites into the almond flour mixture until just combined. This helps to lighten the almond flour mixture.

Add the remaining beaten egg whites to the almond flour mixture and gently fold until the batter is smooth and glossy. Be careful not to overmix, as this can deflate the batter.

Transfer the macaron batter to the prepared piping bag. Pipe small rounds of batter onto the prepared baking sheets, spacing them about 1 inch apart.

Once all the rounds are piped, tap the baking sheets firmly against the counter a few times to release any air bubbles. Let the piped macarons sit at room temperature for about 30 minutes to form a skin. They should feel dry to the touch.

While the macarons are resting, preheat your oven to 300°F (150°C).

Bake the macarons in the preheated oven for 15-18 minutes, or until the tops are set and they have developed feet. The macarons should lift easily off the parchment paper when gently touched.

Remove the macarons from the oven and let them cool completely on the baking sheets.

Once the macarons are cooled, pair them up based on size. Pipe or spoon a small amount of the cooled Swiss chocolate ganache onto the flat side of one macaron shell, then sandwich it with another shell.

Repeat with the remaining macaron shells and ganache.

Place the assembled macarons in an airtight container and refrigerate for at least 24 hours before serving. This allows the flavors to meld and the texture to develop.

Bring the macarons to room temperature before serving. Enjoy these decadent Swiss chocolate macarons as a delightful treat!

Note: Store any leftover macarons in an airtight container in the refrigerator for up to 3-4 days. Allow them to come to room temperature before serving for the best taste and texture.

Swiss Chocolate Bread Pudding

Ingredients:

- 6 cups (approximately 350g) stale bread, cut into cubes
- 200g Swiss dark chocolate, chopped into chunks
- 4 large eggs
- 2 cups (480ml) whole milk
- 1/2 cup (100g) granulated sugar
- 1 teaspoon vanilla extract
- 1/4 teaspoon ground cinnamon
- Pinch of salt
- Butter, for greasing the baking dish
- Whipped cream or vanilla ice cream, for serving (optional)

Instructions:

Preheat your oven to 350°F (175°C). Grease a 9x13-inch (23x33cm) baking dish with butter.
Place the stale bread cubes in the greased baking dish, spreading them out evenly.
Sprinkle the chopped Swiss dark chocolate chunks over the bread cubes, distributing them evenly.
In a large mixing bowl, whisk together the eggs, whole milk, granulated sugar, vanilla extract, ground cinnamon, and a pinch of salt until well combined.
Pour the egg mixture over the bread and chocolate in the baking dish, ensuring that all the bread cubes are soaked in the mixture.
Let the bread pudding sit for about 10-15 minutes to allow the bread to absorb the liquid.
Place the baking dish in the preheated oven and bake for 35-40 minutes, or until the bread pudding is set and the top is golden brown.
Remove the bread pudding from the oven and let it cool slightly before serving.
Serve the Swiss chocolate bread pudding warm, optionally topped with whipped cream or vanilla ice cream for an extra indulgent treat.
Enjoy the comforting and delicious Swiss chocolate bread pudding as a delightful dessert!
Any leftovers can be stored in an airtight container in the refrigerator for up to 3-4 days. Reheat individual servings in the microwave or oven before serving again.

Swiss Chocolate Pots de Crème

Ingredients:

- 200g Swiss dark chocolate, finely chopped
- 1 and 1/2 cups (360ml) heavy cream
- 1/2 cup (120ml) whole milk
- 4 large egg yolks
- 1/4 cup (50g) granulated sugar
- Pinch of salt
- 1 teaspoon vanilla extract
- Whipped cream, for garnish (optional)
- Chocolate shavings or cocoa powder, for garnish (optional)

Instructions:

Preheat your oven to 325°F (160°C). Place six 4-ounce (120ml) ramekins or oven-safe cups in a baking dish.
Place the finely chopped Swiss dark chocolate in a heatproof bowl.
In a saucepan, heat the heavy cream and whole milk over medium heat until it just begins to simmer. Remove from heat.
In a separate mixing bowl, whisk together the egg yolks, granulated sugar, and a pinch of salt until well combined.
Gradually pour the hot cream mixture into the egg yolk mixture, whisking constantly to temper the eggs.
Return the mixture to the saucepan and cook over low heat, stirring constantly, until slightly thickened. Be careful not to let it boil.
Pour the hot custard mixture over the chopped chocolate in the heatproof bowl. Let it sit for a minute to allow the chocolate to melt.
Add the vanilla extract to the chocolate custard mixture and whisk until smooth and well combined.
Strain the chocolate custard mixture through a fine-mesh sieve into a clean bowl to remove any lumps.
Divide the strained chocolate custard mixture evenly among the prepared ramekins or cups.
Carefully pour hot water into the baking dish, being careful not to get any water into the ramekins, until it reaches about halfway up the sides of the ramekins.
Cover the baking dish loosely with aluminum foil.

Place the baking dish in the preheated oven and bake for 30-35 minutes, or until the edges are set but the centers still have a slight jiggle.

Remove the baking dish from the oven and carefully transfer the ramekins to a wire rack to cool completely.

Once cooled, cover the ramekins with plastic wrap and refrigerate for at least 4 hours, or preferably overnight, to set completely.

Before serving, optionally garnish each pot de crème with a dollop of whipped cream and chocolate shavings or cocoa powder.

Serve the Swiss chocolate pots de crème chilled and enjoy the rich and decadent dessert!

Store any leftover pots de crème in the refrigerator for up to 3-4 days.

Swiss Chocolate Dipped Strawberries

Ingredients:

- Fresh strawberries, washed and dried
- 200g Swiss dark chocolate, finely chopped
- Optional toppings (e.g., chopped nuts, shredded coconut, sprinkles)

Instructions:

Line a baking sheet with parchment paper or wax paper.
Place the finely chopped Swiss dark chocolate in a heatproof bowl.
Fill a saucepan with a couple of inches of water and bring it to a simmer over medium-low heat. Place the heatproof bowl with the chocolate on top of the saucepan, ensuring the bottom of the bowl doesn't touch the water. This creates a double boiler.
Stir the chocolate occasionally until it is melted and smooth. Remove the bowl from the heat.
Holding a strawberry by the stem, dip it into the melted chocolate, swirling to coat it evenly. Allow any excess chocolate to drip back into the bowl.
If desired, immediately dip the chocolate-coated strawberry into optional toppings, such as chopped nuts, shredded coconut, or sprinkles.
Place the dipped strawberries onto the prepared baking sheet.
Repeat the dipping process with the remaining strawberries until all are coated in chocolate.
Once all strawberries are dipped and decorated, place the baking sheet in the refrigerator for about 15-20 minutes to allow the chocolate to set.
After the chocolate has set, the strawberries are ready to be served.
Enjoy the decadent Swiss chocolate dipped strawberries as a delightful treat!

Note: These chocolate-dipped strawberries are best enjoyed fresh. Store any leftovers in an airtight container in the refrigerator for up to 1-2 days.

Swiss Chocolate Pancakes

Ingredients:

- 1 cup (125g) all-purpose flour
- 2 tablespoons unsweetened cocoa powder
- 2 tablespoons granulated sugar
- 2 teaspoons baking powder
- 1/4 teaspoon salt
- 1 cup (240ml) milk
- 1 large egg
- 2 tablespoons unsalted butter, melted
- 1 teaspoon vanilla extract
- 100g Swiss dark chocolate, finely chopped
- Butter or oil, for cooking
- Maple syrup, whipped cream, or fresh berries, for serving (optional)

Instructions:

In a large mixing bowl, whisk together the flour, cocoa powder, sugar, baking powder, and salt until well combined.
In a separate bowl, whisk together the milk, egg, melted butter, and vanilla extract until smooth.
Pour the wet ingredients into the dry ingredients and whisk until just combined.
Be careful not to overmix; it's okay if there are a few lumps in the batter.
Gently fold in the chopped Swiss dark chocolate until evenly distributed throughout the batter.
Heat a non-stick skillet or griddle over medium heat and lightly grease with butter or oil.
Pour about 1/4 cup of batter onto the skillet for each pancake. Cook until bubbles form on the surface of the pancake and the edges look set, about 2-3 minutes.
Carefully flip the pancake and cook for an additional 1-2 minutes, or until cooked through and lightly browned on both sides.
Repeat with the remaining batter, greasing the skillet as needed.
Serve the Swiss chocolate pancakes warm, optionally topped with maple syrup, whipped cream, or fresh berries.
Enjoy these deliciously indulgent Swiss chocolate pancakes for breakfast or brunch!

Note: You can customize these pancakes by adding toppings like sliced bananas, chopped nuts, or additional chocolate chips. Feel free to adjust the sweetness to your taste by adding more or less sugar.

Swiss Chocolate Ice Cream

Ingredients:

- 200g Swiss dark chocolate, finely chopped
- 2 cups (480ml) heavy cream
- 1 cup (240ml) whole milk
- 3/4 cup (150g) granulated sugar
- 4 large egg yolks
- 1 teaspoon vanilla extract
- Pinch of salt

Instructions:

Place the finely chopped Swiss dark chocolate in a heatproof bowl.
In a saucepan, heat the heavy cream, whole milk, and granulated sugar over medium heat until it just begins to simmer, stirring occasionally to dissolve the sugar.
In a separate mixing bowl, whisk the egg yolks until smooth.
Slowly pour the hot cream mixture into the egg yolks while whisking constantly to temper the eggs.
Once fully combined, return the mixture to the saucepan and cook over low heat, stirring constantly, until it thickens slightly and coats the back of a spoon. Do not let it boil.
Remove the saucepan from the heat and pour the hot custard mixture over the chopped chocolate in the heatproof bowl.
Let it sit for a minute to allow the chocolate to melt, then whisk until smooth and well combined.
Stir in the vanilla extract and a pinch of salt until fully incorporated.
Strain the chocolate custard mixture through a fine-mesh sieve into a clean bowl to remove any lumps.
Cover the bowl with plastic wrap, pressing it directly onto the surface of the custard to prevent a skin from forming.
Refrigerate the chocolate custard mixture for at least 4 hours, or preferably overnight, until thoroughly chilled.
Once chilled, pour the chocolate custard mixture into an ice cream maker and churn according to the manufacturer's instructions until it reaches a soft-serve consistency.

Transfer the churned ice cream to a freezer-safe container and freeze for at least 4 hours, or until firm.
Serve the Swiss chocolate ice cream scooped into bowls or cones, and enjoy the rich and creamy dessert!
Store any leftover ice cream in an airtight container in the freezer for up to 2 weeks.

Swiss Chocolate Trifle

Ingredients:

For the chocolate cake layer:

- 1 box chocolate cake mix (plus ingredients needed for the cake mix)

For the chocolate pudding layer:

- 2 cups (480ml) whole milk
- 1/2 cup (100g) granulated sugar
- 1/4 cup (30g) unsweetened cocoa powder
- 3 tablespoons cornstarch
- Pinch of salt
- 2 large egg yolks
- 1 teaspoon vanilla extract
- 100g Swiss dark chocolate, finely chopped

For the whipped cream layer:

- 2 cups (480ml) heavy cream
- 1/4 cup (30g) powdered sugar
- 1 teaspoon vanilla extract

For assembly:

- 1 cup (150g) Swiss dark chocolate, chopped into small pieces or chocolate shavings
- Fresh berries for garnish (optional)

Instructions:

Prepare the chocolate cake according to the instructions on the box. Once baked and cooled, cut the cake into small cubes. Set aside.

To make the chocolate pudding layer, in a saucepan, whisk together the whole milk, granulated sugar, cocoa powder, cornstarch, and salt over medium heat until well combined and smooth.

In a separate bowl, whisk the egg yolks. Gradually add a small amount of the hot milk mixture to the egg yolks, whisking constantly, to temper them.

Pour the tempered egg yolk mixture back into the saucepan with the remaining hot milk mixture. Cook over medium heat, stirring constantly, until the mixture thickens and comes to a boil.

Remove the saucepan from the heat and stir in the vanilla extract and chopped Swiss dark chocolate until the chocolate is melted and the pudding is smooth. Let it cool slightly.

To make the whipped cream layer, in a large mixing bowl, whip the heavy cream, powdered sugar, and vanilla extract until stiff peaks form.

To assemble the trifle, layer the chocolate cake cubes in the bottom of a trifle dish or a large glass bowl.

Spoon half of the chocolate pudding over the cake layer, spreading it out evenly.

Spread half of the whipped cream over the chocolate pudding layer.

Repeat the layers with the remaining chocolate cake cubes, chocolate pudding, and whipped cream.

Sprinkle the chopped Swiss dark chocolate or chocolate shavings over the top of the trifle.

Garnish with fresh berries if desired.

Cover and refrigerate the Swiss chocolate trifle for at least 4 hours, or preferably overnight, to allow the flavors to meld and the dessert to set.

Serve the trifle chilled and enjoy the luscious layers of chocolatey goodness!

Store any leftover trifle in the refrigerator for up to 2-3 days.

Swiss Chocolate Biscotti

Ingredients:

- 2 cups (250g) all-purpose flour
- 1/2 cup (50g) unsweetened cocoa powder
- 1 teaspoon baking powder
- 1/4 teaspoon salt
- 1/2 cup (100g) granulated sugar
- 1/2 cup (100g) packed light brown sugar
- 3 large eggs
- 1 teaspoon vanilla extract
- 1/2 cup (100g) Swiss dark chocolate chips or chunks
- 1/2 cup (75g) chopped almonds or hazelnuts (optional)

Instructions:

Preheat your oven to 350°F (175°C). Line a baking sheet with parchment paper.
In a mixing bowl, sift together the all-purpose flour, cocoa powder, baking powder, and salt. Set aside.
In another mixing bowl, beat the granulated sugar, brown sugar, and eggs until light and fluffy.
Stir in the vanilla extract until well combined.
Gradually add the dry ingredients to the wet ingredients, mixing until a dough forms.
Fold in the Swiss dark chocolate chips or chunks and chopped nuts (if using) until evenly distributed throughout the dough.
Divide the dough into two equal portions. Shape each portion into a log, about 12 inches (30cm) long and 2 inches (5cm) wide. Place the logs on the prepared baking sheet, spacing them apart.
Bake in the preheated oven for 25-30 minutes, or until the logs are set and slightly firm to the touch.
Remove the baking sheet from the oven and let the logs cool for about 10 minutes. Reduce the oven temperature to 325°F (160°C).
Using a sharp knife, carefully slice the logs diagonally into 1/2-inch (1.25cm) thick slices.
Place the biscotti slices back on the baking sheet, cut side down, and bake for an additional 10-12 minutes, or until the biscotti are dry and crisp.

Remove from the oven and let the biscotti cool completely on a wire rack.
Once cooled, store the Swiss chocolate biscotti in an airtight container at room temperature.
Serve the biscotti with your favorite hot beverage, such as coffee or tea, and enjoy the rich chocolatey flavor and crunchy texture!
These biscotti can also be dipped in melted chocolate or drizzled with chocolate for extra indulgence.

Swiss Chocolate Lava Cake

Ingredients:

- 4 ounces (113g) Swiss dark chocolate, chopped
- 1/2 cup (113g) unsalted butter
- 2 large eggs
- 2 large egg yolks
- 1/4 cup (50g) granulated sugar
- 1 teaspoon vanilla extract
- 2 tablespoons (15g) all-purpose flour
- Pinch of salt
- Cocoa powder or powdered sugar, for dusting
- Fresh berries and whipped cream, for serving (optional)

Instructions:

Preheat your oven to 425°F (220°C). Grease four ramekins (6-ounce size) with butter and dust them with cocoa powder or powdered sugar. Place them on a baking sheet.

In a heatproof bowl set over a pot of simmering water (double boiler method), melt the chopped Swiss dark chocolate and unsalted butter together, stirring occasionally until smooth. Remove from heat and let it cool slightly.

In a separate mixing bowl, whisk together the eggs, egg yolks, granulated sugar, and vanilla extract until well combined and slightly thickened.

Gradually pour the melted chocolate mixture into the egg mixture, whisking constantly until smooth.

Sift the all-purpose flour and salt into the chocolate mixture. Gently fold the flour and salt into the mixture until just combined. Be careful not to overmix.

Divide the batter evenly among the prepared ramekins, filling each about three-quarters full.

Bake in the preheated oven for 12-14 minutes, or until the edges are set but the center is still slightly jiggly.

Remove the lava cakes from the oven and let them cool in the ramekins for 1-2 minutes.

Carefully run a knife around the edges of each cake to loosen them from the ramekins. Invert each ramekin onto a serving plate and gently tap to release the cake. Be cautious as the ramekins may still be hot.

Dust the tops of the lava cakes with cocoa powder or powdered sugar.
Serve the Swiss chocolate lava cakes immediately, optionally garnished with fresh berries and whipped cream.
Enjoy these decadent lava cakes warm, with their gooey chocolate centers oozing out with every bite!

Swiss Chocolate Granola Bars

Ingredients:

- 2 cups (160g) rolled oats
- 1 cup (80g) unsweetened shredded coconut
- 1/2 cup (60g) chopped nuts (such as almonds, pecans, or walnuts)
- 1/4 cup (30g) flaxseeds or chia seeds
- 1/4 cup (60ml) honey or maple syrup
- 1/4 cup (60ml) coconut oil or melted butter
- 1/4 cup (60g) packed brown sugar
- 1 teaspoon vanilla extract
- Pinch of salt
- 1/2 cup (100g) Swiss dark chocolate chips or chunks

Instructions:

Preheat your oven to 350°F (175°C). Line a 9x9-inch (23x23cm) baking pan with parchment paper, leaving some overhang for easy removal later.

In a large mixing bowl, combine the rolled oats, shredded coconut, chopped nuts, and flaxseeds or chia seeds. Mix well to combine.

In a small saucepan, heat the honey or maple syrup, coconut oil or melted butter, brown sugar, vanilla extract, and salt over medium heat. Stir continuously until the sugar is dissolved and the mixture is smooth.

Pour the wet mixture over the dry ingredients in the mixing bowl. Stir until all the dry ingredients are evenly coated.

Transfer the mixture to the prepared baking pan. Use a spatula or the back of a spoon to press the mixture firmly and evenly into the pan.

Bake in the preheated oven for 20-25 minutes, or until the edges are golden brown.

Remove the pan from the oven and let the granola bars cool completely in the pan.

Once cooled, melt the Swiss dark chocolate chips or chunks in a heatproof bowl set over a pot of simmering water (double boiler method) or in the microwave in short bursts, stirring in between, until smooth.

Drizzle or spread the melted chocolate evenly over the cooled granola bars.

Place the pan in the refrigerator for about 15-20 minutes, or until the chocolate has set.

Once the chocolate has set, use the parchment paper overhang to lift the granola bars out of the pan. Place them on a cutting board and cut into bars of your desired size.

Store the Swiss chocolate granola bars in an airtight container at room temperature for up to one week, or in the refrigerator for longer shelf life.

Enjoy these delicious and nutritious granola bars as a snack or dessert on the go!

Swiss Chocolate Pudding

Ingredients:

- 1/2 cup (100g) granulated sugar
- 1/4 cup (30g) unsweetened cocoa powder
- 3 tablespoons cornstarch
- Pinch of salt
- 2 cups (480ml) whole milk
- 100g Swiss dark chocolate, chopped
- 1 teaspoon vanilla extract
- Whipped cream or chocolate shavings for garnish (optional)

Instructions:

In a medium saucepan, whisk together the granulated sugar, cocoa powder, cornstarch, and salt until well combined.
Gradually whisk in the whole milk until smooth and there are no lumps.
Place the saucepan over medium heat and cook the mixture, stirring constantly, until it thickens and comes to a gentle boil.
Reduce the heat to low and continue to cook, stirring constantly, for another 2 minutes until the pudding is thickened.
Remove the saucepan from the heat and stir in the chopped Swiss dark chocolate until it is completely melted and the pudding is smooth.
Stir in the vanilla extract until well combined.
If you prefer a smoother texture, you can strain the pudding through a fine-mesh sieve to remove any lumps.
Divide the chocolate pudding into serving dishes or ramekins.
Cover the surface of each pudding with plastic wrap to prevent a skin from forming.
Refrigerate the chocolate pudding for at least 2-3 hours, or until chilled and set.
Before serving, optionally garnish each pudding with a dollop of whipped cream or chocolate shavings.
Enjoy the rich and creamy Swiss chocolate pudding as a delightful dessert!
Store any leftover pudding in the refrigerator for up to 2-3 days.

Swiss Chocolate Banana Bread

Ingredients:

- 1 and 1/2 cups (180g) all-purpose flour
- 1/2 cup (50g) unsweetened cocoa powder
- 1 teaspoon baking soda
- 1/2 teaspoon baking powder
- 1/4 teaspoon salt
- 3 ripe bananas, mashed (about 1 and 1/2 cups)
- 1/2 cup (100g) granulated sugar
- 1/2 cup (100g) packed light brown sugar
- 1/2 cup (120ml) vegetable oil or melted coconut oil
- 2 large eggs
- 1 teaspoon vanilla extract
- 1 cup (175g) Swiss dark chocolate chips or chunks

Instructions:

Preheat your oven to 350°F (175°C). Grease a 9x5-inch (23x13cm) loaf pan or line it with parchment paper.

In a large mixing bowl, sift together the all-purpose flour, cocoa powder, baking soda, baking powder, and salt. Set aside.

In another mixing bowl, mash the ripe bananas with a fork until smooth.

Add the granulated sugar, brown sugar, vegetable oil or melted coconut oil, eggs, and vanilla extract to the mashed bananas. Mix until well combined.

Gradually add the dry ingredients to the wet ingredients, mixing until just combined. Be careful not to overmix.

Fold in the Swiss dark chocolate chips or chunks until evenly distributed throughout the batter.

Pour the batter into the prepared loaf pan and spread it out evenly.

Bake in the preheated oven for 50-60 minutes, or until a toothpick inserted into the center of the bread comes out clean or with a few moist crumbs.

If the top of the bread starts to brown too quickly, you can cover it loosely with aluminum foil halfway through baking.

Once baked, remove the banana bread from the oven and let it cool in the pan for about 10 minutes.

After 10 minutes, transfer the banana bread to a wire rack to cool completely.

Once cooled, slice the Swiss chocolate banana bread and serve.

Enjoy the deliciously moist and chocolatey banana bread as a snack or dessert! Store any leftover bread in an airtight container at room temperature for up to 3 days, or in the refrigerator for longer shelf life.

Swiss Chocolate Cannoli

Ingredients:

For the cannoli shells:

- 1 cup (125g) all-purpose flour
- 2 tablespoons granulated sugar
- 1/4 teaspoon salt
- 2 tablespoons unsalted butter, softened
- 1/4 cup (60ml) white wine or Marsala wine
- Vegetable oil, for frying

For the chocolate filling:

- 1 cup (240ml) heavy cream
- 200g Swiss dark chocolate, chopped
- 1/4 cup (30g) powdered sugar
- 1 teaspoon vanilla extract
- 1/2 cup (60g) chopped nuts (such as pistachios or almonds), optional
- Powdered sugar, for dusting

Instructions:

In a mixing bowl, combine the all-purpose flour, granulated sugar, and salt. Cut in the softened butter using a pastry cutter or fork until the mixture resembles coarse crumbs.

Gradually add the white wine or Marsala wine, mixing until a dough forms. Knead the dough lightly until smooth.

Wrap the dough in plastic wrap and let it rest at room temperature for at least 30 minutes.

On a lightly floured surface, roll out the dough to about 1/8 inch thickness. Use a round cutter (about 4 inches in diameter) to cut out circles from the dough.

Wrap each dough circle around a cannoli tube, overlapping the edges slightly, and seal them with a dab of egg white.

Heat vegetable oil in a deep fryer or heavy-bottomed pot to 350°F (175°C). Fry the cannoli shells, a few at a time, until golden brown and crispy, about 2-3 minutes.

Use tongs to carefully remove them from the oil and place them on a paper towel-lined plate to drain and cool.

In a heatproof bowl, combine the heavy cream and chopped Swiss dark chocolate. Microwave in short bursts or melt over a double boiler until the chocolate is melted and the mixture is smooth. Let it cool slightly.

Once cooled, whisk in the powdered sugar and vanilla extract until well combined. If desired, stir in the chopped nuts.

Fill a piping bag fitted with a large star tip (or simply use a spoon) with the chocolate filling.

Carefully pipe the chocolate filling into each end of the cooled cannoli shells, filling them completely.

Dust the filled cannoli with powdered sugar and, if desired, sprinkle with additional chopped nuts.

Serve the Swiss chocolate cannoli immediately and enjoy the decadent treat!

Any leftover filled cannoli can be stored in an airtight container in the refrigerator for up to 1-2 days. Note that the shells may soften slightly over time, so it's best to fill them shortly before serving.

Swiss Chocolate Marshmallows

Ingredients:

- 3 tablespoons unflavored gelatin (about 3 packets)
- 1 cup (240ml) cold water, divided
- 2 cups (400g) granulated sugar
- 2/3 cup (160ml) light corn syrup
- 1/4 teaspoon salt
- 1 tablespoon vanilla extract
- 1/2 cup (85g) Swiss dark chocolate, chopped
- Powdered sugar, for dusting

Instructions:

In the bowl of a stand mixer fitted with the whisk attachment, combine the gelatin and 1/2 cup of cold water. Let it sit for about 10 minutes to soften.

In a medium saucepan, combine the granulated sugar, corn syrup, salt, and the remaining 1/2 cup of cold water. Stir over medium heat until the sugar is dissolved.

Increase the heat to medium-high and let the mixture come to a boil. Once boiling, cook without stirring until a candy thermometer reads 240°F (115°C), also known as the soft ball stage.

With the stand mixer on low speed, slowly pour the hot sugar syrup into the gelatin mixture, being careful to avoid splattering. Once all the syrup is added, increase the speed to high and beat until the mixture is very thick and fluffy, about 10-15 minutes. The mixture should be cool to the touch.

While the mixture is beating, melt the Swiss dark chocolate in a heatproof bowl set over a pot of simmering water (double boiler method) or in the microwave in short bursts, stirring in between, until smooth. Let it cool slightly.

Once the marshmallow mixture is thick and fluffy, add the vanilla extract and melted chocolate. Beat until well combined.

Grease a 9x13-inch (23x33cm) baking pan and dust it generously with powdered sugar.

Pour the marshmallow mixture into the prepared pan and smooth the top with a spatula.

Dust the top of the marshmallow mixture with more powdered sugar.

Let the marshmallows set at room temperature for at least 4 hours, or preferably overnight, until firm and set.

Once set, use a sharp knife or cookie cutters to cut the marshmallows into squares or shapes of your desired size.

Dust the cut edges of the marshmallows with more powdered sugar to prevent sticking.

Store the Swiss chocolate marshmallows in an airtight container at room temperature for up to 1-2 weeks.

Enjoy these homemade Swiss chocolate marshmallows on their own, in hot chocolate, or use them in your favorite recipes!

Swiss Chocolate Rice Krispie Treats

Ingredients:

- 3 tablespoons unflavored gelatin (about 3 packets)
- 1 cup (240ml) cold water, divided
- 2 cups (400g) granulated sugar
- 2/3 cup (160ml) light corn syrup
- 1/4 teaspoon salt
- 1 tablespoon vanilla extract
- 1/2 cup (85g) Swiss dark chocolate, chopped
- Powdered sugar, for dusting

Instructions:

In the bowl of a stand mixer fitted with the whisk attachment, combine the gelatin and 1/2 cup of cold water. Let it sit for about 10 minutes to soften.

In a medium saucepan, combine the granulated sugar, corn syrup, salt, and the remaining 1/2 cup of cold water. Stir over medium heat until the sugar is dissolved.

Increase the heat to medium-high and let the mixture come to a boil. Once boiling, cook without stirring until a candy thermometer reads 240°F (115°C), also known as the soft ball stage.

With the stand mixer on low speed, slowly pour the hot sugar syrup into the gelatin mixture, being careful to avoid splattering. Once all the syrup is added, increase the speed to high and beat until the mixture is very thick and fluffy, about 10-15 minutes. The mixture should be cool to the touch.

While the mixture is beating, melt the Swiss dark chocolate in a heatproof bowl set over a pot of simmering water (double boiler method) or in the microwave in short bursts, stirring in between, until smooth. Let it cool slightly.

Once the marshmallow mixture is thick and fluffy, add the vanilla extract and melted chocolate. Beat until well combined.

Grease a 9x13-inch (23x33cm) baking pan and dust it generously with powdered sugar.

Pour the marshmallow mixture into the prepared pan and smooth the top with a spatula.

Dust the top of the marshmallow mixture with more powdered sugar.

Let the marshmallows set at room temperature for at least 4 hours, or preferably overnight, until firm and set.

Once set, use a sharp knife or cookie cutters to cut the marshmallows into squares or shapes of your desired size.

Dust the cut edges of the marshmallows with more powdered sugar to prevent sticking.

Store the Swiss chocolate marshmallows in an airtight container at room temperature for up to 1-2 weeks.

Enjoy these homemade Swiss chocolate marshmallows on their own, in hot chocolate, or use them in your favorite recipes!

Swiss Chocolate Panna Cotta

Ingredients:

- 2 cups (480ml) heavy cream
- 1/2 cup (120ml) whole milk
- 1/2 cup (100g) granulated sugar
- 200g Swiss dark chocolate, chopped
- 2 teaspoons unflavored gelatin powder
- 2 tablespoons cold water
- 1 teaspoon vanilla extract
- Pinch of salt

Instructions:

In a saucepan, combine the heavy cream, whole milk, and granulated sugar. Heat the mixture over medium heat, stirring occasionally, until it starts to simmer. Remove from heat.
Add the chopped Swiss dark chocolate to the hot cream mixture and stir until the chocolate is completely melted and the mixture is smooth.
In a small bowl, sprinkle the gelatin powder over the cold water and let it sit for about 5 minutes to soften.
After the gelatin has softened, stir it into the warm chocolate mixture until fully dissolved.
Stir in the vanilla extract and a pinch of salt until well combined.
Divide the chocolate mixture evenly among 4-6 serving glasses or ramekins.
Place the glasses or ramekins in the refrigerator and chill the panna cotta until set, about 4 hours or overnight.
Once set, the panna cotta should be firm to the touch.
Serve the Swiss chocolate panna cotta chilled, optionally garnished with whipped cream, chocolate shavings, or fresh berries.
Enjoy the rich and creamy dessert with its decadent Swiss chocolate flavor!
Store any leftover panna cotta in the refrigerator for up to 2-3 days.

Swiss Chocolate Caramel Slice

Ingredients:

For the base:

- 1 cup (125g) all-purpose flour
- 1/2 cup (50g) unsweetened cocoa powder
- 1/2 cup (100g) granulated sugar
- 1/2 cup (115g) unsalted butter, melted

For the caramel filling:

- 1 can (14 ounces or 397g) sweetened condensed milk
- 1/2 cup (100g) light brown sugar, packed
- 1/4 cup (60g) unsalted butter
- 2 tablespoons golden syrup or corn syrup
- Pinch of salt

For the chocolate topping:

- 200g Swiss dark chocolate, chopped
- 2 tablespoons unsalted butter

Instructions:

Preheat your oven to 350°F (175°C). Grease and line a 9x9-inch (23x23cm) square baking pan with parchment paper, leaving an overhang on the sides for easy removal.
In a mixing bowl, combine the all-purpose flour, cocoa powder, and granulated sugar for the base. Stir in the melted butter until well combined.
Press the mixture evenly into the bottom of the prepared baking pan.
Bake the base in the preheated oven for 15-18 minutes, or until set. Remove from the oven and let it cool slightly.
While the base is cooling, prepare the caramel filling. In a saucepan, combine the sweetened condensed milk, light brown sugar, unsalted butter, golden syrup, and a pinch of salt. Cook over medium-low heat, stirring constantly, until the mixture thickens and turns a caramel color, about 8-10 minutes.

Pour the caramel filling over the cooled base, spreading it out evenly. Return the pan to the oven and bake for an additional 10-12 minutes, or until the caramel is bubbling and slightly darkened.

Remove the pan from the oven and let it cool completely in the pan on a wire rack.

Once the caramel slice has cooled, prepare the chocolate topping. In a heatproof bowl set over a pot of simmering water (double boiler method), melt the Swiss dark chocolate and unsalted butter together until smooth.

Pour the melted chocolate over the cooled caramel layer, spreading it out evenly with a spatula.

Refrigerate the caramel slice for at least 2 hours, or until the chocolate topping is set.

Once set, use the parchment paper overhang to lift the caramel slice out of the pan. Place it on a cutting board and cut into squares or bars.

Serve the Swiss chocolate caramel slice chilled and enjoy the irresistible combination of chocolate and caramel flavors!

Store any leftover caramel slice in an airtight container in the refrigerator for up to 1 week.

Swiss Chocolate Nut Clusters

Ingredients:

- 200g Swiss dark chocolate, chopped
- 1 cup (150g) mixed nuts (such as almonds, cashews, walnuts, or pecans)
- 1/4 cup (35g) dried cranberries or raisins (optional)
- Sea salt flakes (optional)

Instructions:

Line a baking sheet with parchment paper or a silicone baking mat.
In a heatproof bowl, melt the Swiss dark chocolate either in the microwave in short bursts, stirring in between, or using a double boiler method until smooth and fully melted.
Once the chocolate is melted, remove the bowl from the heat and let it cool slightly.
Stir in the mixed nuts and dried cranberries or raisins (if using) into the melted chocolate until they are evenly coated.
Using a spoon or cookie scoop, drop spoonfuls of the chocolate-nut mixture onto the prepared baking sheet, spacing them apart.
If desired, sprinkle each cluster with a pinch of sea salt flakes for a salty-sweet flavor contrast.
Place the baking sheet in the refrigerator for about 30 minutes, or until the chocolate has set and the nut clusters are firm.
Once set, remove the nut clusters from the refrigerator and transfer them to an airtight container for storage.
Store the Swiss chocolate nut clusters in a cool, dry place at room temperature for up to 1 week.
Enjoy these delicious and satisfying chocolate nut clusters as a snack or dessert!

Feel free to customize this recipe by using your favorite combination of nuts and dried fruits, or adding a sprinkle of spices such as cinnamon or chili powder for extra flavor.

Swiss Chocolate Crepes

Ingredients:

For the crepes:

- 1 cup (125g) all-purpose flour
- 2 tablespoons unsweetened cocoa powder
- 2 tablespoons granulated sugar
- Pinch of salt
- 2 large eggs
- 1 cup (240ml) milk
- 1/4 cup (60ml) water
- 2 tablespoons unsalted butter, melted
- 1 teaspoon vanilla extract

For the filling:

- 200g Swiss dark chocolate, chopped
- 1/2 cup (120ml) heavy cream
- 1 tablespoon unsalted butter
- Powdered sugar, for dusting (optional)
- Fresh berries or whipped cream, for serving (optional)

Instructions:

In a mixing bowl, whisk together the all-purpose flour, cocoa powder, granulated sugar, and salt.
In a separate bowl, whisk the eggs, milk, water, melted butter, and vanilla extract until well combined.
Gradually add the wet ingredients to the dry ingredients, whisking constantly, until a smooth batter forms. Let the batter rest for about 15-20 minutes.
While the batter is resting, prepare the chocolate filling. In a heatproof bowl, combine the chopped Swiss dark chocolate, heavy cream, and unsalted butter. Microwave in short bursts or melt over a double boiler until the chocolate is melted and the mixture is smooth. Set aside to cool slightly.

Heat a non-stick skillet or crepe pan over medium heat. Lightly grease the skillet with butter or oil.

Pour a small ladleful of the crepe batter into the center of the skillet and immediately swirl the pan to spread the batter thinly and evenly.

Cook the crepe for about 1-2 minutes, or until the edges start to lift and the bottom is lightly browned. Use a spatula to flip the crepe and cook for another 1-2 minutes on the other side.

Transfer the cooked crepe to a plate and cover with a clean kitchen towel to keep warm. Repeat with the remaining batter, greasing the skillet as needed, until all the batter is used.

Once all the crepes are cooked, spoon some of the chocolate filling onto each crepe and spread it out evenly.

Fold the crepes into quarters or roll them up, and place them on serving plates.

Dust the Swiss chocolate crepes with powdered sugar, if desired, and serve with fresh berries or whipped cream on the side.

Enjoy these decadent Swiss chocolate crepes as a delicious breakfast, brunch, or dessert option!

Feel free to customize the filling by adding sliced bananas, chopped nuts, or a drizzle of caramel sauce for extra flavor.

Swiss Chocolate Toffee

Ingredients:

- 1 cup (200g) granulated sugar
- 1 cup (225g) unsalted butter
- 1 tablespoon water
- Pinch of salt
- 200g Swiss dark chocolate, chopped
- 1/2 cup (60g) chopped nuts (such as almonds or pecans), optional

Instructions:

Line a baking sheet with parchment paper or a silicone baking mat. Set aside.
In a heavy-bottomed saucepan, combine the granulated sugar, unsalted butter, water, and a pinch of salt.
Cook the mixture over medium heat, stirring constantly with a wooden spoon, until the sugar dissolves and the butter melts.
Once the mixture starts to boil, reduce the heat to medium-low and continue to cook, stirring occasionally, until it reaches a deep golden brown color and registers 300°F (150°C) on a candy thermometer. This is the hard crack stage.
Remove the saucepan from the heat and immediately pour the hot toffee onto the prepared baking sheet, spreading it out evenly with a spatula.
Let the toffee cool and set at room temperature for about 5-10 minutes.
While the toffee is still warm but beginning to set, sprinkle the chopped Swiss dark chocolate evenly over the surface.
Let the chocolate sit for a minute or two to soften, then use a spatula to spread it out evenly over the toffee.
If desired, sprinkle the chopped nuts over the melted chocolate layer, pressing them lightly into the chocolate.
Place the baking sheet in the refrigerator for about 30 minutes, or until the chocolate is set and the toffee is firm.
Once set, break the Swiss chocolate toffee into bite-sized pieces.
Store the toffee in an airtight container at room temperature for up to 2 weeks.
Enjoy the deliciously crunchy and chocolatey Swiss chocolate toffee as a sweet treat or gift it to friends and family!

This recipe can be customized by adding additional toppings such as sea salt, shredded coconut, or dried fruit for extra flavor and texture.

Swiss Chocolate Coconut Balls

Ingredients:

- 200g Swiss dark chocolate, chopped
- 1 cup (90g) unsweetened shredded coconut
- 1/2 cup (120ml) sweetened condensed milk
- 1 teaspoon vanilla extract
- Pinch of salt
- Extra shredded coconut, cocoa powder, or chopped nuts for coating (optional)

Instructions:

In a heatproof bowl set over a pot of simmering water (double boiler method), melt the Swiss dark chocolate until smooth. Alternatively, you can melt the chocolate in the microwave in short bursts, stirring in between, until fully melted.
In a separate mixing bowl, combine the unsweetened shredded coconut, sweetened condensed milk, vanilla extract, and a pinch of salt.
Pour the melted chocolate over the coconut mixture and stir until well combined. Cover the bowl with plastic wrap and refrigerate the mixture for about 30 minutes to 1 hour, or until it is firm enough to handle.
Once chilled, use a spoon or cookie scoop to portion out the chocolate-coconut mixture and roll it into balls about 1 inch in diameter. If the mixture is too sticky to handle, you can lightly grease your hands with coconut oil or butter.
If desired, roll the chocolate coconut balls in extra shredded coconut, cocoa powder, or chopped nuts for coating.
Place the coated balls on a baking sheet lined with parchment paper and refrigerate for another 30 minutes to allow them to firm up.
Once firm, the Swiss chocolate coconut balls are ready to be served.
Enjoy these delicious and decadent treats as a snack or dessert!
Store any leftover chocolate coconut balls in an airtight container in the refrigerator for up to 1 week.

Swiss Chocolate Chia Pudding

Ingredients:

- 1/4 cup (40g) chia seeds
- 1 cup (240ml) unsweetened almond milk (or any milk of your choice)
- 2 tablespoons unsweetened cocoa powder
- 2 tablespoons maple syrup or honey
- 1/2 teaspoon vanilla extract
- 50g Swiss dark chocolate, chopped (optional, for extra richness)
- Toppings of your choice (such as fresh berries, sliced bananas, shredded coconut, chopped nuts, or whipped cream)

Instructions:

In a mixing bowl, combine the chia seeds, unsweetened almond milk, unsweetened cocoa powder, maple syrup or honey, and vanilla extract. Whisk until well combined.
If you prefer a smoother texture, you can blend the mixture in a blender until smooth. This step is optional.
If using, stir in the chopped Swiss dark chocolate for extra richness.
Cover the bowl and refrigerate the chocolate chia pudding mixture for at least 2 hours, or preferably overnight, to allow the chia seeds to absorb the liquid and thicken.
After the pudding has chilled and thickened, give it a good stir to break up any clumps and evenly distribute the chocolate and chia seeds.
Divide the chocolate chia pudding into serving bowls or jars.
Add your favorite toppings, such as fresh berries, sliced bananas, shredded coconut, chopped nuts, or a dollop of whipped cream.
Serve the Swiss chocolate chia pudding immediately and enjoy the creamy and indulgent treat!
Any leftover chocolate chia pudding can be stored in an airtight container in the refrigerator for up to 3-4 days. Stir well before serving.

Feel free to adjust the sweetness level by adding more or less maple syrup or honey according to your preference. You can also customize the flavor by adding a dash of cinnamon or a pinch of sea salt for extra depth.

Swiss Chocolate Caramel Popcorn

Ingredients:

For the popcorn:

- 1/2 cup (100g) popcorn kernels
- 3 tablespoons vegetable oil
- Salt, to taste

For the caramel:

- 1 cup (200g) granulated sugar
- 1/4 cup (60ml) water
- 1/4 cup (60ml) heavy cream
- 2 tablespoons unsalted butter
- Pinch of salt

For the Swiss chocolate drizzle:

- 100g Swiss dark chocolate, chopped
- 1 tablespoon unsalted butter

Instructions:

Preheat your oven to 250°F (120°C). Line a baking sheet with parchment paper or a silicone baking mat. Set aside.

In a large pot with a lid, heat the vegetable oil over medium-high heat. Add the popcorn kernels and cover the pot with the lid. Once the kernels start popping, gently shake the pot occasionally to ensure even popping. Remove from heat when the popping slows down to once every few seconds. Be careful not to burn the popcorn. Season the popcorn with salt to taste and transfer it to a large mixing bowl. Remove any unpopped kernels.

In a saucepan, combine the granulated sugar and water for the caramel. Cook over medium heat, stirring occasionally, until the sugar dissolves.

Once the sugar has dissolved, stop stirring and let the mixture come to a boil. Continue to cook without stirring until it turns a deep amber color, swirling the pan occasionally to ensure even caramelization. This should take about 5-7 minutes.

Remove the saucepan from the heat and carefully pour in the heavy cream while whisking constantly. Be cautious as the mixture will bubble up vigorously.

Return the saucepan to the heat and simmer the caramel for another 1-2 minutes, stirring constantly, until it thickens slightly.

Remove the saucepan from the heat and stir in the unsalted butter and a pinch of salt until fully incorporated.

Pour the caramel over the popcorn in the mixing bowl and use a spatula to gently toss until the popcorn is evenly coated with caramel.

Spread the caramel-coated popcorn onto the prepared baking sheet in an even layer.

Bake in the preheated oven for 45-60 minutes, stirring every 15 minutes, until the caramel coating is dry and crisp.

While the caramel popcorn is cooling, prepare the Swiss chocolate drizzle. In a heatproof bowl set over a pot of simmering water (double boiler method), melt the Swiss dark chocolate and unsalted butter together until smooth.

Drizzle the melted chocolate over the cooled caramel popcorn.

Allow the chocolate drizzle to set at room temperature or speed up the process by placing the baking sheet in the refrigerator for about 15-20 minutes.

Once the chocolate drizzle has set, break the caramel popcorn into clusters and serve.

Enjoy the irresistible combination of sweet caramel, crunchy popcorn, and rich Swiss chocolate!

Store any leftover caramel popcorn in an airtight container at room temperature for up to 1 week.

Swiss Chocolate Raspberry Tart

Ingredients:

For the crust:

- 1 and 1/4 cups (155g) all-purpose flour
- 1/4 cup (30g) unsweetened cocoa powder
- 1/4 cup (50g) granulated sugar
- 1/2 cup (115g) unsalted butter, cold and cut into small cubes
- 1 large egg yolk
- 1-2 tablespoons cold water

For the chocolate filling:

- 200g Swiss dark chocolate, chopped
- 1 cup (240ml) heavy cream
- 2 tablespoons unsalted butter, softened
- 1 teaspoon vanilla extract

For the raspberry topping:

- 2 cups (300g) fresh raspberries
- 2 tablespoons raspberry jam
- Powdered sugar, for dusting (optional)

Instructions:

Preheat your oven to 375°F (190°C). Grease a 9-inch (23cm) tart pan with a removable bottom.
In a food processor, combine the all-purpose flour, unsweetened cocoa powder, and granulated sugar for the crust. Pulse a few times to mix.
Add the cold cubed butter to the food processor and pulse until the mixture resembles coarse crumbs.
Add the egg yolk and 1 tablespoon of cold water to the mixture. Pulse until the dough starts to come together. If the dough seems too dry, add another tablespoon of cold water.

Turn the dough out onto a lightly floured surface and knead it gently until it forms a smooth ball.

Roll out the dough into a circle slightly larger than your tart pan. Carefully transfer the dough to the prepared tart pan and press it into the bottom and up the sides. Trim off any excess dough.

Prick the bottom of the crust with a fork to prevent it from puffing up during baking.

Line the crust with parchment paper and fill it with pie weights or dried beans.

Bake the crust in the preheated oven for 15 minutes. Remove the parchment paper and weights, and bake for an additional 5-7 minutes, or until the crust is set and dry.

Remove the crust from the oven and let it cool completely in the pan on a wire rack.

While the crust is cooling, prepare the chocolate filling. In a heatproof bowl set over a pot of simmering water (double boiler method), melt the Swiss dark chocolate until smooth. Stir in the heavy cream, softened butter, and vanilla extract until well combined and smooth.

Pour the chocolate filling into the cooled tart crust and spread it out evenly with a spatula.

Arrange the fresh raspberries on top of the chocolate filling in a single layer, pressing them lightly into the filling.

In a small saucepan, heat the raspberry jam over low heat until it becomes liquid. Brush the melted jam over the raspberries to glaze them.

Refrigerate the tart for at least 1-2 hours, or until the chocolate filling is set.

Once set, remove the tart from the refrigerator and carefully remove it from the tart pan.

If desired, dust the tart with powdered sugar before serving.

Slice and serve the Swiss chocolate raspberry tart chilled, and enjoy the decadent combination of rich chocolate and tart raspberries!

Store any leftover tart in the refrigerator for up to 2-3 days.

Swiss Chocolate Oatmeal Cookies

Ingredients:

- 1 cup (125g) all-purpose flour
- 1/2 teaspoon baking soda
- 1/4 teaspoon salt
- 1/2 cup (115g) unsalted butter, softened
- 1/2 cup (100g) granulated sugar
- 1/2 cup (100g) packed light brown sugar
- 1 large egg
- 1 teaspoon vanilla extract
- 1 and 1/2 cups (150g) old-fashioned oats
- 1 cup (175g) Swiss dark chocolate chips or chunks

Instructions:

Preheat your oven to 350°F (175°C). Line baking sheets with parchment paper or silicone baking mats.
In a mixing bowl, whisk together the all-purpose flour, baking soda, and salt. Set aside.
In a large mixing bowl, cream together the softened unsalted butter, granulated sugar, and packed light brown sugar until light and fluffy.
Beat in the egg and vanilla extract until well combined.
Gradually add the dry ingredients to the wet ingredients, mixing until just combined.
Stir in the old-fashioned oats and Swiss dark chocolate chips or chunks until evenly distributed throughout the dough.
Drop spoonfuls of dough onto the prepared baking sheets, leaving some space between each cookie for spreading.
Bake in the preheated oven for 10-12 minutes, or until the edges are lightly golden brown.
Remove the cookies from the oven and let them cool on the baking sheets for a few minutes before transferring them to wire racks to cool completely.
Once cooled, serve and enjoy these delicious Swiss chocolate oatmeal cookies with a glass of milk or your favorite hot beverage!
Store any leftover cookies in an airtight container at room temperature for up to 1 week.

Feel free to customize these cookies by adding chopped nuts (such as walnuts or pecans), dried fruits (such as raisins or cranberries), or shredded coconut for extra flavor and texture.

Swiss Chocolate Hazelnut Spread

Ingredients:

- 1 cup (150g) hazelnuts
- 200g Swiss dark chocolate, chopped
- 3 tablespoons cocoa powder
- 1/2 cup (120ml) maple syrup or honey
- 2 tablespoons coconut oil, melted
- 1 teaspoon vanilla extract
- Pinch of salt

Instructions:

Preheat your oven to 350°F (175°C). Spread the hazelnuts in a single layer on a baking sheet and toast them in the preheated oven for 10-12 minutes, or until fragrant and lightly browned. Remove from the oven and let them cool slightly. Once cooled, transfer the toasted hazelnuts to a clean kitchen towel. Rub the hazelnuts in the towel to remove as much of the skins as possible.
In a food processor, grind the toasted hazelnuts until they form a smooth paste, scraping down the sides of the bowl as needed. This process may take several minutes, depending on the power of your food processor.
In a heatproof bowl set over a pot of simmering water (double boiler method), melt the Swiss dark chocolate until smooth.
Add the melted chocolate, cocoa powder, maple syrup or honey, melted coconut oil, vanilla extract, and a pinch of salt to the hazelnut paste in the food processor. Process the mixture until everything is well combined and smooth, scraping down the sides of the bowl as needed.
Taste the chocolate hazelnut spread and adjust the sweetness or saltiness to your liking, adding more maple syrup or salt if desired.
Transfer the chocolate hazelnut spread to a clean jar or airtight container.
Allow the spread to cool completely before sealing the container.
Store the Swiss chocolate hazelnut spread in the refrigerator for up to 2 weeks.
Before serving, let it come to room temperature for easier spreading.
Enjoy the creamy and indulgent Swiss chocolate hazelnut spread on toast, pancakes, waffles, fruit, or simply enjoy it straight from the spoon!
Note: The texture of the spread may thicken slightly when refrigerated, but it will soften again at room temperature.

Swiss Chocolate Mint Brownies

Ingredients:

For the brownie layer:

- 1/2 cup (115g) unsalted butter
- 200g Swiss dark chocolate, chopped
- 3/4 cup (150g) granulated sugar
- 2 large eggs
- 1 teaspoon vanilla extract
- 1/2 cup (65g) all-purpose flour
- 1/4 teaspoon salt

For the mint layer:

- 1 and 1/2 cups (180g) powdered sugar
- 3 tablespoons unsalted butter, softened
- 1 tablespoon milk
- 1/2 teaspoon peppermint extract
- Green food coloring (optional)

For the chocolate ganache:

- 100g Swiss dark chocolate, chopped
- 1/4 cup (60ml) heavy cream
- 1 tablespoon unsalted butter

Instructions:

Preheat your oven to 350°F (175°C). Grease and line an 8x8-inch (20x20cm) square baking pan with parchment paper, leaving an overhang on the sides for easy removal.

In a heatproof bowl set over a pot of simmering water (double boiler method), melt the unsalted butter and Swiss dark chocolate together until smooth. Alternatively, you can melt them in the microwave in short bursts, stirring in between, until fully melted.

Remove the bowl from the heat and let the mixture cool slightly.

Stir in the granulated sugar, eggs, and vanilla extract until well combined.

Gradually add the all-purpose flour and salt to the chocolate mixture, stirring until just combined. Be careful not to overmix.

Pour the brownie batter into the prepared baking pan and spread it out evenly with a spatula.

Bake in the preheated oven for 20-25 minutes, or until the top is set and a toothpick inserted into the center comes out with a few moist crumbs.

Remove the brownies from the oven and let them cool completely in the pan on a wire rack.

While the brownies are cooling, prepare the mint layer. In a mixing bowl, beat together the powdered sugar, softened unsalted butter, milk, peppermint extract, and green food coloring (if using) until smooth and creamy. Adjust the consistency with more powdered sugar or milk if needed.

Spread the mint layer evenly over the cooled brownies in the pan.

In a heatproof bowl set over a pot of simmering water (double boiler method), melt the Swiss dark chocolate, heavy cream, and unsalted butter together until smooth, stirring constantly.

Pour the chocolate ganache over the mint layer, spreading it out evenly with a spatula.

Refrigerate the brownies for at least 1 hour, or until the ganache is set.

Once set, use the parchment paper overhang to lift the brownies out of the pan and transfer them to a cutting board.

Cut the brownies into squares and serve.

Enjoy these decadent Swiss chocolate mint brownies as a delightful treat!

Swiss Chocolate Almond Butter Cups

Ingredients:

For the almond butter filling:

- 1/2 cup (120g) almond butter
- 2 tablespoons maple syrup or honey
- 1/4 teaspoon vanilla extract
- Pinch of salt

For the chocolate coating:

- 200g Swiss dark chocolate, chopped
- 1 tablespoon coconut oil

For decoration (optional):

- Sliced almonds
- Sea salt flakes

Instructions:

Line a mini muffin tin with mini paper or silicone cupcake liners. Set aside.
In a small bowl, mix together the almond butter, maple syrup or honey, vanilla extract, and a pinch of salt until smooth and well combined. Set aside.
In a heatproof bowl set over a pot of simmering water (double boiler method), melt the Swiss dark chocolate and coconut oil together until smooth, stirring constantly.
Once melted, remove the chocolate mixture from the heat.
Spoon a small amount of melted chocolate into the bottom of each lined mini muffin cup, using about half of the chocolate.
Gently tap the muffin tin on the counter to spread the chocolate evenly and remove any air bubbles.
Place the muffin tin in the refrigerator for about 10-15 minutes, or until the chocolate has set.
Once the chocolate has set, spoon a small amount of almond butter filling into each cup, using about a teaspoon for each cup.
Flatten and smooth out the almond butter filling with the back of a spoon.

Spoon the remaining melted chocolate over the almond butter filling in each cup, covering it completely and smoothing the top with a spoon.

If desired, sprinkle sliced almonds or sea salt flakes on top of the chocolate before it sets.

Return the muffin tin to the refrigerator and chill the almond butter cups for at least 30 minutes, or until the chocolate is firm.

Once set, remove the almond butter cups from the muffin tin and peel away the paper or silicone liners.

Serve and enjoy these delicious Swiss chocolate almond butter cups as a delightful treat!

Store any leftover almond butter cups in an airtight container in the refrigerator for up to 1 week. Make sure to let them come to room temperature before serving for the best texture.

Swiss Chocolate Shortbread

Ingredients:

- 1 cup (225g) unsalted butter, softened
- 1/2 cup (60g) powdered sugar
- 2 cups (250g) all-purpose flour
- 1/4 cup (30g) unsweetened cocoa powder
- 1/4 teaspoon salt
- 100g Swiss dark chocolate, chopped (for dipping, optional)

Instructions:

Preheat your oven to 350°F (175°C). Line a baking sheet with parchment paper or a silicone baking mat.
In a large mixing bowl, cream together the softened unsalted butter and powdered sugar until light and fluffy.
In a separate bowl, sift together the all-purpose flour, unsweetened cocoa powder, and salt.
Gradually add the dry ingredients to the creamed butter and sugar mixture, mixing until a dough forms. Be careful not to overmix.
Turn the dough out onto a lightly floured surface and knead it gently until smooth. Roll out the dough to about 1/4 inch (6mm) thickness.
Use cookie cutters to cut out shapes from the dough. You can use any shape you like, such as rounds, squares, or rectangles.
Place the cut-out cookies onto the prepared baking sheet, spacing them apart. Prick the tops of the cookies with a fork to create a decorative pattern and to prevent them from puffing up during baking.
Bake in the preheated oven for 10-12 minutes, or until the cookies are set and the edges are lightly golden brown.
Remove the cookies from the oven and let them cool on the baking sheet for a few minutes before transferring them to a wire rack to cool completely.
Optional: Once the cookies are cooled, melt the Swiss dark chocolate in a heatproof bowl set over a pot of simmering water (double boiler method) or in the microwave in short bursts, stirring in between, until fully melted. Dip the cooled cookies halfway into the melted chocolate and place them back on the parchment paper to set.
Allow the chocolate to set completely before serving or storing the cookies.

Enjoy these delicious Swiss chocolate shortbread cookies as a delightful treat with a cup of tea or coffee!

Store any leftover cookies in an airtight container at room temperature for up to 1 week.

Swiss Chocolate Liqueur Truffles

Ingredients:

For the truffle filling:

- 200g Swiss dark chocolate, chopped
- 1/2 cup (120ml) heavy cream
- 2 tablespoons unsalted butter
- 2 tablespoons chocolate liqueur (such as Kahlua or Baileys)
- 1/2 teaspoon vanilla extract

For coating:

- Cocoa powder, powdered sugar, finely chopped nuts, or melted chocolate for coating

Instructions:

Place the chopped Swiss dark chocolate in a heatproof bowl.
In a small saucepan, heat the heavy cream over medium heat until it just starts to simmer. Remove from heat immediately.
Pour the hot cream over the chopped chocolate and let it sit for 1-2 minutes to soften the chocolate.
Gently stir the chocolate and cream together until smooth and fully combined.
Add the unsalted butter, chocolate liqueur, and vanilla extract to the chocolate mixture. Stir until the butter is melted and the mixture is smooth.
Cover the bowl with plastic wrap and refrigerate the truffle filling for at least 2 hours, or until it is firm enough to handle.
Once the truffle filling is chilled and firm, use a spoon or small scoop to portion out small balls of the mixture. Roll each portion between your palms to form smooth balls. Place the rolled truffles on a parchment-lined baking sheet and return them to the refrigerator for 15-20 minutes to chill.
Prepare the coating for the truffles. You can roll them in cocoa powder, powdered sugar, finely chopped nuts, or dip them in melted chocolate.

If dipping the truffles in melted chocolate, melt the chocolate in a heatproof bowl set over a pot of simmering water (double boiler method) or in the microwave in short bursts, stirring in between, until smooth.

Remove the chilled truffles from the refrigerator. Using a fork or dipping tool, dip each truffle into the melted chocolate, coating it completely. Tap off any excess chocolate and place the dipped truffle back on the parchment-lined baking sheet.

If desired, sprinkle the dipped truffles with additional toppings such as cocoa powder, powdered sugar, or chopped nuts before the chocolate sets.

Repeat the dipping process with the remaining truffles.

Once all the truffles are coated and decorated, refrigerate them for another 15-20 minutes to allow the chocolate coating to set.

Once set, transfer the Swiss chocolate liqueur truffles to an airtight container for storage.

Enjoy these decadent homemade truffles as a delicious treat or gift them to friends and family!

Store the truffles in the refrigerator for up to 2 weeks. Let them come to room temperature before serving for the best flavor and texture.

Swiss Chocolate Brioche

Ingredients:

For the brioche dough:

- 3 cups (375g) all-purpose flour
- 1/4 cup (50g) granulated sugar
- 1 teaspoon salt
- 1 tablespoon active dry yeast
- 1/2 cup (120ml) warm milk
- 3 large eggs, at room temperature
- 1/2 cup (115g) unsalted butter, softened

For the chocolate filling:

- 200g Swiss dark chocolate, chopped
- 1/4 cup (50g) granulated sugar
- 1/4 cup (60ml) heavy cream
- 2 tablespoons unsalted butter
- 1 teaspoon vanilla extract

For the egg wash:

- 1 egg, beaten
- 1 tablespoon milk

Instructions:

In a small bowl, dissolve the active dry yeast in warm milk. Let it sit for about 5-10 minutes, or until foamy.
In a large mixing bowl or the bowl of a stand mixer fitted with a dough hook attachment, combine the flour, sugar, and salt.
Add the yeast mixture and eggs to the dry ingredients. Mix on low speed until the dough starts to come together.
Gradually add the softened unsalted butter, one tablespoon at a time, while continuing to mix on low speed.
Once all the butter has been added, increase the speed to medium and knead the dough for about 8-10 minutes, or until it is smooth, elastic, and pulls away from the sides of the bowl.

Place the dough in a lightly greased bowl, cover it with plastic wrap or a clean kitchen towel, and let it rise in a warm place for about 1-2 hours, or until doubled in size.

While the dough is rising, prepare the chocolate filling. In a heatproof bowl set over a pot of simmering water (double boiler method), melt the Swiss dark chocolate, granulated sugar, heavy cream, unsalted butter, and vanilla extract together until smooth and well combined. Remove from heat and let it cool slightly.

Once the dough has doubled in size, punch it down and turn it out onto a lightly floured surface.

Roll out the dough into a large rectangle, about 1/4 inch (6mm) thick.

Spread the chocolate filling evenly over the surface of the dough, leaving a small border around the edges.

Starting from one long side, tightly roll up the dough into a log.

Using a sharp knife, cut the log into slices, about 1 inch (2.5cm) thick.

Place the slices in a greased baking dish or on a parchment-lined baking sheet, leaving some space between each slice for rising.

Cover the brioche rolls loosely with plastic wrap or a clean kitchen towel and let them rise for another 30-45 minutes, or until puffy.

Preheat your oven to 350°F (175°C).

In a small bowl, whisk together the beaten egg and milk to make the egg wash.

Brush the tops of the risen brioche rolls with the egg wash.

Bake the Swiss chocolate brioche in the preheated oven for 20-25 minutes, or until golden brown and cooked through.

Remove from the oven and let the brioche cool slightly before serving.

Enjoy the indulgent Swiss chocolate brioche warm or at room temperature, with a cup of coffee or tea!

Store any leftover brioche rolls in an airtight container at room temperature for up to 2 days. Reheat before serving if desired.

Swiss Chocolate Cherry Clafoutis

Ingredients:

- 1 cup (150g) fresh cherries, pitted
- 1/2 cup (100g) granulated sugar
- 3 large eggs
- 1 cup (240ml) whole milk
- 1/2 cup (120ml) heavy cream
- 1/2 cup (60g) all-purpose flour
- 1/4 cup (25g) unsweetened cocoa powder
- 1 teaspoon vanilla extract
- Pinch of salt
- Swiss dark chocolate chips or chunks (optional, for extra chocolate flavor)

Instructions:

Preheat your oven to 350°F (175°C). Grease a 9-inch (23cm) round baking dish with butter or non-stick cooking spray.
Arrange the pitted cherries in a single layer in the bottom of the prepared baking dish.
In a mixing bowl, whisk together the granulated sugar and eggs until light and frothy.
Gradually whisk in the whole milk, heavy cream, vanilla extract, and a pinch of salt until well combined.
Sift in the all-purpose flour and unsweetened cocoa powder into the wet ingredients. Whisk until the batter is smooth and free of lumps.
If using, sprinkle Swiss dark chocolate chips or chunks over the cherries in the baking dish.
Pour the batter over the cherries and chocolate in the baking dish, covering them evenly.
Place the baking dish in the preheated oven and bake for 35-40 minutes, or until the clafoutis is set and puffed up around the edges. The center may still be slightly jiggly.
Remove the clafoutis from the oven and let it cool for a few minutes before serving.
Serve the Swiss chocolate cherry clafoutis warm or at room temperature, dusted with powdered sugar if desired.
Enjoy this decadent dessert as a delightful treat for any occasion!

Store any leftover clafoutis in the refrigerator for up to 2-3 days. Reheat before serving if desired.

Swiss Chocolate Cinnamon Rolls

Ingredients:

For the dough:

- 1 cup (240ml) whole milk
- 1/4 cup (50g) granulated sugar
- 1 packet (7g) active dry yeast
- 1/2 cup (115g) unsalted butter, melted and cooled
- 2 large eggs
- 4 cups (500g) all-purpose flour
- 1 teaspoon salt

For the filling:

- 1/2 cup (100g) granulated sugar
- 1/2 cup (100g) brown sugar
- 2 tablespoons unsweetened cocoa powder
- 2 teaspoons ground cinnamon
- 1/4 cup (55g) unsalted butter, softened
- 100g Swiss dark chocolate, chopped

For the cream cheese glaze:

- 4 oz (115g) cream cheese, softened
- 1/4 cup (55g) unsalted butter, softened
- 1 cup (120g) powdered sugar
- 1/2 teaspoon vanilla extract
- 2-3 tablespoons whole milk

Instructions:

In a small saucepan, heat the whole milk until it reaches about 110°F (43°C). Remove from heat and transfer to a large mixing bowl.
Stir in the granulated sugar and sprinkle the active dry yeast over the warm milk. Let it sit for about 5-10 minutes, or until foamy.

Add the melted and cooled unsalted butter and eggs to the yeast mixture. Mix until well combined.

Gradually add the all-purpose flour and salt to the wet ingredients, stirring until a dough forms.

Turn the dough out onto a lightly floured surface and knead it for about 5-7 minutes, or until smooth and elastic.

Place the dough in a greased bowl, cover it with plastic wrap or a clean kitchen towel, and let it rise in a warm place for about 1-2 hours, or until doubled in size.

While the dough is rising, prepare the filling. In a small bowl, mix together the granulated sugar, brown sugar, unsweetened cocoa powder, and ground cinnamon.

Once the dough has doubled in size, punch it down and roll it out into a large rectangle, about 1/4 inch (6mm) thick.

Spread the softened unsalted butter evenly over the surface of the dough.

Sprinkle the cinnamon sugar mixture evenly over the buttered dough, then sprinkle the chopped Swiss dark chocolate on top.

Starting from one long side, tightly roll up the dough into a log.

Use a sharp knife to cut the log into slices, about 1-1.5 inches (2.5-3.8cm) thick.

Place the slices in a greased baking dish or on a parchment-lined baking sheet, leaving some space between each roll for rising.

Cover the rolls loosely with plastic wrap or a clean kitchen towel and let them rise for another 30-45 minutes, or until puffy.

Preheat your oven to 350°F (175°C).

Bake the cinnamon rolls in the preheated oven for 20-25 minutes, or until golden brown and cooked through.

While the rolls are baking, prepare the cream cheese glaze. In a mixing bowl, beat together the softened cream cheese and unsalted butter until smooth.

Gradually add the powdered sugar and vanilla extract, mixing until smooth.

Thin the glaze with 2-3 tablespoons of whole milk until you reach your desired consistency.

Once the cinnamon rolls are done baking, remove them from the oven and let them cool for a few minutes.

Drizzle the cream cheese glaze over the warm cinnamon rolls.

Serve the Swiss chocolate cinnamon rolls warm and enjoy the delicious combination of chocolate, cinnamon, and cream cheese!

Store any leftover cinnamon rolls in an airtight container at room temperature for up to 2-3 days. Reheat before serving if desired.

Swiss Chocolate Pecan Pie

Ingredients:

For the crust:

- 1 9-inch (23 cm) pre-made pie crust, unbaked

For the filling:

- 1 cup (175g) Swiss dark chocolate chips or chunks
- 1 and 1/2 cups (180g) pecan halves
- 3 large eggs
- 1 cup (200g) granulated sugar
- 1 cup (240ml) dark corn syrup
- 1/4 cup (60ml) unsalted butter, melted
- 1 teaspoon vanilla extract
- 1/4 teaspoon salt

Instructions:

Preheat your oven to 350°F (175°C). Place the unbaked pie crust in a 9-inch (23 cm) pie dish and crimp the edges as desired.
Spread the Swiss dark chocolate chips or chunks evenly over the bottom of the pie crust. Arrange the pecan halves on top of the chocolate layer.
In a mixing bowl, beat the eggs lightly with a fork or whisk.
Add the granulated sugar, dark corn syrup, melted unsalted butter, vanilla extract, and salt to the beaten eggs. Stir until well combined.
Pour the filling mixture over the pecans and chocolate in the pie crust, making sure to distribute it evenly.
Carefully transfer the pie to the preheated oven and bake for 50-60 minutes, or until the filling is set and slightly puffed up. The center may still jiggle slightly when gently shaken.
If the edges of the crust start to brown too quickly during baking, you can cover them with aluminum foil to prevent burning.
Once baked, remove the pie from the oven and let it cool completely on a wire rack before slicing and serving.

Serve the Swiss chocolate pecan pie at room temperature or slightly warmed, optionally with a dollop of whipped cream or a scoop of vanilla ice cream.
Enjoy this decadent and indulgent dessert with friends and family during holidays or special occasions!
Store any leftover pie in the refrigerator for up to 3-4 days. Allow it to come to room temperature before serving leftovers.

Swiss Chocolate Banana Split

Ingredients:

- 3 ripe bananas
- Swiss dark chocolate, melted
- Vanilla ice cream
- Whipped cream
- Maraschino cherries
- Chopped nuts (such as almonds, walnuts, or pecans)
- Sprinkles (optional)

Instructions:

Peel the bananas and slice each one in half lengthwise.
Arrange the banana halves in a serving dish or on a plate, placing them side by side.
Drizzle the melted Swiss dark chocolate over the banana halves.
Place a scoop of vanilla ice cream on top of each banana half.
Garnish with a dollop of whipped cream on top of the ice cream.
Top each banana split with a maraschino cherry.
Sprinkle chopped nuts over the banana splits for added crunch and flavor.
Optionally, decorate with sprinkles for a colorful touch.
Serve the Swiss chocolate banana splits immediately and enjoy!
Feel free to customize your banana splits with additional toppings such as chocolate syrup, caramel sauce, or sliced strawberries.
Serve and enjoy this delicious and indulgent dessert with friends and family!

Swiss Chocolate Peanut Butter Bars

Ingredients:

For the base:

- 1 and 1/2 cups (180g) graham cracker crumbs
- 1/2 cup (115g) unsalted butter, melted
- 1/4 cup (50g) granulated sugar

For the peanut butter layer:

- 1 cup (250g) creamy peanut butter
- 1/2 cup (115g) unsalted butter, softened
- 2 cups (250g) powdered sugar
- 1 teaspoon vanilla extract

For the chocolate topping:

- 200g Swiss dark chocolate, chopped
- 1/4 cup (60ml) heavy cream
- 2 tablespoons unsalted butter

Instructions:

Preheat your oven to 350°F (175°C). Grease a 9x9-inch (23x23cm) square baking pan and line it with parchment paper, leaving an overhang on the sides for easy removal.
In a mixing bowl, combine the graham cracker crumbs, melted unsalted butter, and granulated sugar for the base. Mix until the crumbs are evenly coated.
Press the mixture firmly into the bottom of the prepared baking pan to form an even layer.
Bake the crust in the preheated oven for 10 minutes. Remove from the oven and let it cool slightly.
While the crust is cooling, prepare the peanut butter layer. In a mixing bowl, beat together the creamy peanut butter, softened unsalted butter, powdered sugar, and vanilla extract until smooth and creamy.
Spread the peanut butter mixture evenly over the cooled crust in the baking pan.

In a heatproof bowl set over a pot of simmering water (double boiler method), melt the Swiss dark chocolate, heavy cream, and unsalted butter together until smooth, stirring constantly.

Pour the melted chocolate mixture over the peanut butter layer in the baking pan, spreading it out evenly with a spatula.

Refrigerate the bars for at least 1-2 hours, or until the chocolate topping is set.

Once set, use the parchment paper overhang to lift the bars out of the pan. Place them on a cutting board and slice into bars or squares.

Serve and enjoy these decadent Swiss chocolate peanut butter bars as a delicious treat!

Store any leftover bars in an airtight container in the refrigerator for up to 1 week. Let them come to room temperature before serving for the best texture.